FOLLOW YOUR DREAMS

Terry Daniels

FOLLOW YOUR DREAMS

ISBN :9781450590563

Published by:
Dynasty Inc. Publishing
5424 Central Avenue
Charlotte, North Carolina

704.563.4520

Author Signing Page

Acknowledgments

Chara Fortson, Shayna Hampton,

& Reitha Morrison

FOLLOW YOUR DREAM

Terry Daniels

Follow Your Dream

Follow your dream
Is for only you
To know that your main goal
And to understand
It will be true

To know and to believe
That there will be no other direction
To give all that you have
And to complete it at your satisfaction

There will be only one path
And only one road that you will see
Because once you past the end of it
Then you would know that you are free

Because this is something
That you will see to the end
A drive that you will have
The only outcome is to win

Because the word number two
Does not even exists
One is the only number
And it is at the tip of the list

Because you would have poured
All of your heart, love, and soul
To reach that mountain top
That you set as your goal

To accomplish something
That no one else thought that you could
A real feeling all inside
That you knew that you would

As I think of Our Father
I can understand what he did mean
For his son, to sacrifice his life
Just to follow His Dream

I Am So Afraid

I am so afraid
Of what I am about to see
This vision that I had
Is headed right here to me

You see when it first started
I never thought it would come true
I forgot who I had asked
I forgot it was you

Because how could I have ever dreamed
Of something just like this
I could only come from you my father
And it is not any wish

You see miracles do happen
But you must truly believe
Just ask Our God
And then you will receive

You see my Father I do know
This is not all about me
It's me belaying some words
On how to be free

To be able to accept
All the things that I have heard
To understand your only son
And to believe in his true words

For us to be with you
And have an everlasting life
For us to acknowledge and understand
In our savior Jesus Christ

You see my father, I do know
All the roads that he paved
Even though I am aware of all of this
Still Why Am I So Afraid?

Terry Daniels

Rest And Relaxation

Rest and relaxation
What does it really mean?
This thing will be real
But it would seem like a dream

To wake up each day
With not a worry in the world
To not worry about money
Diamonds, gold or pearls

Because everything that you want
Is right there in your sight
No matter when you would get the urge for it
Morning, noon or night

To have a place
That you can't explain
To have accepted a true love
That was not given in vain

To understand what was said
And will forever be true
To know of a deep passion
That was always meant for you

For your life to have a new beginning
That did start on this day
To know that he heard all your thoughts
Every time you did pray

To welcome you to a home
That is furnished in nothing but love
To accept his warmest greetings
As you entered here above

As I see you my child
You have had a long destination
So grab a seat by me and start enjoying your
Rest and Relaxation

I Surrender

I surrender
Yes I have finally given up
The battle with things I thought I wanted
The fight was very tough

But these were things
That would do me no good
It's not that I needed them
It was just that I could

You see yes I do know
The right from the wrongs
I do know the straight path
That will take me back home

Away from this world
That gets worse every day
I wonder my father
Does it help me when I pray?

I see so much darkness
And it seems like it will never end
I'm trying to hold on to my sanity
Because I will not let the devil win

Because you have never ever
Left me behind
No matter through all of my burdens
Your sun continued to shine

I know that you are with me
And you are always close by
Because whenever I feel lonely
There is always that beautiful blue sky

If this world would except the thought
That you are our protector and defender
If we would just relinquish everything
And say Father I Surrender

Terry Daniels

My God Is Real

My God Is Real
And this is so true
To create this whole world
For me and for you

For us to understand
That there is only one true love
That all powers and glory
Does come from above

To give us a world
So that we could live
To show us a love
That only he could give

From the moment you were born
And for the rest of your life
Me, your father
Will forever be insight

I will stay with you my child
Forever and always
I will be by your side
Through all of your days

Now remember the reason
That I was sent
For all of God's children
All they must do is repent

To give me your heart
Your mind and soul
With all three of them together
You have paid your toll

To my home in paradise
You have earned this deal
My child, my baby your
God is Real

I Wonder

I wonder what it will be like
When I finally meet you
Everything that I have heard everything I saw
Will they be true?

How did you get this power?
Where did it come from?
I know about you
I heard about your Son

There is so much to ask
And I don't know where to start
But every time I think of you
A strange feeling enters my heart

It's just like a flutter
That runs all over me
A sensation so unusual
A feeling of totally free

It's like there's nothing around
That can give me any fear
Just that one little simple thought
That knows that you are here

I know that my soul
That you value so much
I could not be me
Without your special touch

Because there is no way
That this world would exist
Everything that you have created
You sealed it with your kiss

The trees that grows oh so high
The roaring of the thunder
Everything that lives, My Father
No more will I Wonder

Terry Daniels

Believe In Me

Believe in me
Because I am right here
I am always by your side
So have no fear

This is your time
That you must understand
I am your father
I am no man

I see this burden
That is weighing on your mind
Just believe in Me
And peace you will find

My Child I see
All the pains in your heart
Just give them all to Me
Prayer is a good start

I know that there are times
That you think you are all alone
But remember My Child
I am always at home

A voice that will speak to you
Any time that you wish
Remember My Child
You are on top of My list

I am right here with you
I have never left your side
I gave my life
So that your soul would not die

I promise to this world
Eternal life to be free
All that I ask of you is just to
Believe In Me

Why Am I Going Through This

Why am I going through this?
What did I do wrong?
Every time I turn around
I hear the same old song

You see I am here for your purpose
Anything you say I will do
Because my purpose in life
Is to love and serve you

Because you are my creator
You gave me my life's breath
And I have said so many times
You are the only one who can give me my death

Now this is the time in my life
That I should be happy and free
Because all of the thoughts on my mind
Is pleasing and loving thee

He is our father
Who has loved us oh so well?
He is our savior
That doesn't want us to go to hell

But this is not what I am worried about
Right now it is no concern
Because as long as I live for my father
And remember everything I have learned

Now My Children please listen
To everything that I say
I will always be with you
Forever and a day

Now My Children just try to understand
As I deliver it with a kiss
Baby you are my chosen Angel that's
Why you are going through this

Terry Daniels

Life After Death

Life after death
What does this really mean?
Something very unusual
But this is not a dream

To wake up to some thing
That you could never imagine
A place you've never been
A brand new horizon

To feel that finally
You are at a place that cares
A presence of a love
That wants only to share

To be with you personally
To have a friend that is true
To know that someone
Really enjoys being with you

For you to think back
And to wonder why now
All the times you needed comfort
The many times you were down

Now all of a sudden
Your whole world has changed
To see only happiness
And to have no feelings of pain

There is laughter all around
And smiles you can't believe
There are blessings every where
Just reach out to receive

To pray to be here
To this place that you should not have left
Now you can understand our father's plan that there is
Life After Death

Why

Why is a word
That I don't understand
The answer to that word
Does not come from man

Man could not tell you
Right from wrong
There is only one place
That one place should be home

A place from here
A place so far away
A place so free
All you must do is just pray

To ask for a life
A life without sin
Whenever you have problems
There is always a hand that will lend

To help you through troubles
That will come to us all
Deliverance all around
All you have to do is just call

To the end of your journey
To the end of your race
To know what your life was
To except what you face

See this was God's reason
And this was His plan
When you finally meet the Father
Then you will know where you stand

As I look all around
I see this beautiful blue sky
The home of Our Father
And the answer to
Why

Terry Daniels

Thin Line

Thin line to me
What is it to you?
Your last chance in life
For you to choose

Right or wrong
Make sure you are correct
Because the one that you pick
Forever your future is will effect

Because this is for real
And it will be your last time
On which side of the fence
Will your destiny you find

You see this is your future
And your life is at stake
Whatever you decide
An everlasting choice you will make

So let's make it simple
Either your freedom or a cell
But what I am talking about seriously
Either heaven or hell

You see this is your life
And only you know what you need
Do you want what is real?
Or just accept being deceived

My friends please listen
I prefer the truth and the life
See I have no second thoughts
I will turn it all over to my Jesus Christ

So please listen very carefully
And go with it thoroughly through your mind
Because without the Father in your life
You are most defiantly walking on a
Thin Line

Wishing On A Star

Wishing on a star
Now what does that do?
Something that is personal
Something that's for you

You see each day is different
And every two things aren't the same
Because one day could bring sunny skies
An the next one could be rain

But dreams are only dreams
And they very seldom com true
For this to be your life line
There will only be a few

Please understand what I am saying
This world is not for long
At the end of your visit here
There's a place you will call home

Because when you get to this place
It will be all that you want
Because everything is right here
And there is no reason for you to hurt

Because this is my dream
For my children to be by my side
No matter what I asked of you
You kindly tried to abide

You see this is only the beginning
Of everything that you have heard
To you my child I will whisper
But you can hear each and every word

So welcome home My Child
Because you have come so far
You see you have earned this journey without
Wish On A Star

Terry Daniels

Peace Out

Peace out to me
Means over with and done
Either I was the loser
Or either I won

This phrase will stop
Anything that you are doing
Even if you are traveling
You will eventually stop moving

Where ever there's a start
There is also an ending
As long as there is life around
There will always be some sinning

This is the way
That our lives will revolve
Whenever there are problems near by
There is a place where they can be solved

A place so free and open
This place so far away
But anytime it's needed
All you have to do is just pray

When all options are closed
And there is nowhere else to turn
There is a lesson right in front of you
And so easy to learn

It will teach you the fundamentals
Of the way your life should be lived
It will bless you with a loving spirit
And a compassion to want to give

But now as my life is coming to an end
My mind will have no doubts
As I give my soul to My Father
And to this world
Peace Out

Humble Me

Humble me please
For I can understand
Humble me honestly
So I can accept your plan

For me to realize
The trueness of your grace
For me to know
Why I had to run this race

What is the reason?
That I must join in
What is the prize?
What do I win?

As you ask this question
I will never tell you a lie
Your pains and your struggles
That I see from My sky

The love that I have for you
I cannot show you on earth
Your real home with Me
That you were given before your birth

See when I make promises
You must believe they are true
The things you do not see
Are things I can put in view?

See when I ask you to give me
Your heart soul and mind
At the end of your rainbow
My kingdom you will find

Because I am the answer
And I hold the life's key
Just do one little thing just
Humble Before Me

Terry Daniels

Awesome

Awesome is a word
That there is nothing to compare
Something so unheard of
That should make you aware

Aware of the things
That you may take for granted
Not to understand a power
That will soon demand it

When it gets turned on
It will do things never seen
Something so unusual
It will make you think it's a dream

But this is for real
And there are no words to describe
This thing that I am speaking of
Made ever thing alive

With every breath of air
That you absorb within
There is a love all around you
That will forgive all your sins

You see this is a world
Built on truth, love and grace
At the end of your journey here
You will see only our Father's Face

A Father that will love you
No matter whatever you do wrong
A love that will stay with you
Until you return back home

As you look all around
You see the trees, the birds and the flowers in blossom
And the one that made all of this possible
Our Father isn't He Awesome

No Respect

No respect
What a powerful phrase
To understand what it means
It could put you in a daze

Because this means to me
To treat someone as you want to be treated
If that is not the case
Then you should feel like you've been defeated

Because this is a world
That everyone is not the same
You see when one person gets hurt
No one else should feel the pain

Now this is why I am so glad
Of this important thing
That there is only one real love
And that love is Our King

A Father that knows me
Much better than I know myself
A Father who will love me
Through sickness and through health

He has given us life
When no one else could
He will stand right by your side
When no one else would

No matter the time of day
Where ever the place
When you think there is no way out
Any trouble he will erase

As I think of everything He has done for us
Not one thing did he neglect
He has given us all the love in the world
And we still give Him
No Respect

Terry Daniels

You Have Got To Believe

You have got to believe
In everything He said he will do
You have got to believe
His whole purpose is loving you

To take him as His word
You must understand
This is our father
And this is no man

You see man can say one thing
And then do another
His truth that is oh so real
And so very easy to discover

No matter what ever you may ask
Rather it is yes, or rather it is no
The answer that you will get from Him
Only the good path he will show

Now My Children just listen
And accept what I am saying
There is nothing in this whole world I can't change
So all you have to do is start praying

Because I Am the Creator
Of everything that exit
From this World that you see right now
From a dark and dreary mist

You see when everything seems there's no way out
And you think you cannot make it
That is when you should truly have Faith
And know I am the only one to erase it

Just give Me the chance to share My Love
Just open your arms to receive
Now your burdens has disappeared
Only because You
Believed

How Do I Love You

How do I love you?
Let me count the ways
Each moment of each hour
Each second I do pray

To seek a new vision
That I could only have imagined
Something not real for me
Only another fantasy

To reach out and to touch
For something that is really not there
A glimmer of hope
Happiness that I could share

I can only dream
Of an illusion that does not exist
A passion that has avoided me
No lips for me to kiss

How can I find happiness?
When I've searched this whole world through
So my luck has finally changed
And brought me straight to you

Now I am so excited
And I've learned how to smile
This journey that I have traveled
And for you it was worth each mile

Now you are right here
And it's been such a very long time
As you hold me in your arms
And tell me that you are mine

As I think of this one thought
Anything worth waiting for is true
With you constantly on my mind that's
How I Do Love You

Terry Daniels

Sugar Pie

Sugar pie is a lady
What more can I say
The kind of a lady
That you must see each day

Because every day starts with her
From morning until night
Every second spent with this princess
Is such a special delight

A presence of fresh air
That will sooth your mind and soul
Her love without any doubt
Is more valuable than any gold

There is no man worthy
Of a woman of this degree
She is a flower so genuine
And a violet oh so free

To think of a true love
For her I can't compare
Anytime spent with this lady
Like an hour is just like a blair

Because this angel that I speak of
Is every love potion in one?
One sip of her liquid
And your heart is completely done

The things she may say
And the things that you may see
Just one kiss from her lips
And you will give her your key

From the first time I met her
I acknowledged there are angels from the sky
This dessert from another world yes my
Sugar Pie

Heaven Made

Heaven made
So what else can be said?
Not a thought, not a wish
Not a book to be read

When anything happens
That comes from above
There is one thing for sure
And it is true love

Because the Father would not give you
Anything second best
Any gift from Him
Will always be Heavenly Blessed

As I look at this true Angel
All I can think of is my life
To wake up each morning
And to know that she is My Wife

For me to love her faithfully
It would be so easy for me to do
For the first time in my life
I would have found a love that is true

Because with her by my side
All of my heart I will give
This present from Our Father
In paradise we will live

To learn about each other
Each second is not enough
The longer I'm away from her
I'm lost without her touch

You see with my father blessing
All my needs have been paid
Because this blessing that was given to me
Is most defiantly Heaven Made

Terry Daniels

I Want To Help

I want to help
Now what can I do?
All the things I see wrong
And yes I do have a clue

As I see things that are bad
To me it really does hurt
I know I can pray to You
And I know that this does work

But Father I am only human
And your time is not mine
I am looking for something quick
And so easy to find

I see the pains
That these people do endure
If only I had the tools
For a fast and easy cure

But Father I do know
That this is not Your desire
I must trust and believe in your words
And know I can't go any higher

Heaven is the place
Where all things are resolved
Without your answer
There is nothing that can be solved

Father you are the one
Who loves us the most
And Father I cannot wait
To have You as My Host

I know this is so different
And I am speaking for myself
I know I am of your own image
So it is not wrong for me
To Want To Help

Eat, Drink And Be Merry

Eat, drink and be merry
Is this what I really feel?
To have this food for thought
This should be truly real

This should be a time
That we all should be glad
These times that I speak of
There is no room to be sad

For this joyous occasion
The sun should be bright and so clear
This is the time for true happiness
And no room for any type of fear

The birds should sing so cheerful
The flowers all in bloom
The sun shines so brightly
This time should be high noon

Something is going to happen
That will change the whole course of man
See this will be the start
Of Our Father's Master Plan

He knew when it would began
He understand when it would start
He accepted this great burden
He gave freely from his heart

To give up his life
So that the only way we could win
He gave up His own blood
He died for Our sins

This is our Lord Jesus
Who has died for all our troubles and worries?
As I know of my Father's suffering
I could not Eat, Drink and be Merry

Terry Daniels

You Ain't Seen Nothing Yet

You ain't seen nothing yet
Because I'm just now beginning
My first step was so easy
I just stop sinning

Once that was all over
My whole world began to change
The sun came out bright
And dried up all of the rain

Because everything that I thought
That I could control
Was all in my head
And not on My Father's Road

The path that He gave
To all of his Children
A direction so simple
And a guaranteed deliverance

Because whatever He touch
It's all ready pure gold
A life to live forever
A place to rest your soul

Because when your life is over
And your body back to the ground
Your soul will return back to Our Father
To live for eternity heavenly bound

Because when that day comes
And trust me it will
A new life will begin
And a new love you will feel

Because now as I sat back and realized
That all my hardships were just a test
Since I gave them all to My Father, just watch
You Ain't Seen Nothing Yet

Let Go And Let God

Let go and let God
Why is this so true?
Because all of his love
Was meant totally for you

The worries that you carry
The troubles on your mind
The burden that you possess
A relief you must truly find

You see it will not go away
But just closing of your eyes
It will appear to you again
Only in a different disguise

You see this is the real world
And things are not always as you like
But there's a love all around
And will always be insight

It is there no matter what
Through your good and your bad
It smiles when you are happy
It consoles you when you are sad

There is nothing in your life
That could ever turn it away
Only one simple thing to do
Is just kneel down and pray

You see tomorrow is not tomorrow
And today is just for today
But the love of Our Father
Is forever and always

So whatever your struggles are
And your road seems long and hard
The answers to all of your problems just
Let go and let God

Terry Daniels

An Eye For An Eye

An eye for an eye
A tooth for a tooth
You should have known this
Since you were a youth

You see the things that you thought
And the things that you know
Will show you the way
That your directions should go

You see this is the time
That you should understand
This is for real
And you must act like a man

To take on every problem
That will come day by day
To confront anything
And do it face to face

You see this is a problem
That has only one solution
To do away with it completely
And eliminate all your confusion

But was this the correct path
That your life should be lived
All your burdens and trouble
To the Father you should give

Because He is the answer
To all unhappiness that comes your way
When you think everything is wrong
Just kneel down and pray

You see as I have grown older
I ask myself why
So I gave it all to my God
And let him decide rather an Eye for an Eye

Player Hating

Player hating
How can this be true?
Stop looking at me
And start looking at you

Because the way that I live
Is for only me to decide
No matter what I do
There will be nothing for me to hide

As I look at my life
I see only one goal
To achieve a great success
A position I will continue to hold

I will strive for nothing
That is not better than the best
I must achieve top quality
And I will accept no less

You see this is what I am about
And this is what I want
I will go through any extreme
I will continue my relentless hunt

To follow my true passion
To continue on my search
To take any step that I need
To find what really will work

Sometimes my body gets very tired
And the expressions on my face will show
But I understand what I must do
To get to the end of my road

Now for all of you people that don't have dreams
Well just continue to keep on waiting
Because I will fulfill my destiny
So you all just stop Player Hating

Terry Daniels

Darkness

Darkness is here
And now you are all alone
Now you wonder to yourself
Which place did you call home

You see there should be no doubts
In your mind, heart, and soul
Because you knew what the stakes were
And should have followed the right road

Because you had a decision
Of which home to reside
A choice that was in your face
A promise you can't deny

Because when the Father says something
His word is forever true
And the love in His heart
Will always be for you

But the Devil as I have seen him
He wants heartaches and pains
He doesn't like the sunshine
And He enjoys all kind of rain

He does not care anything
About you or your life
The only thing that will make Him happy
Are all your troubles and strives

Now just sit back and think to yourself
Who would you prefer for a host?
Someone that likes tortures and suffering
Or someone who knows the Holy Ghost

Now just imagine the rest of your life
Not because of your brightness or smartness
Which could have been so easy to choose
Because only a fool would want Darkness

O' For The Grace Of God, Go I

O' for the grace of God go I
It's not what I see
It's not what I heard
All that I know is this person could be me

As I look at him struggling
Through life day by day
I wonder to myself
Does he know how to pray?

Because the Father that I know of
Would be there by His side
He would protect him and be with him
And would always be his guide

No matter what problems
That you will endure
There will forever be a love for you
And you can rest assured

You see there is no burden
That this world could go through
That the blood of our Jesus
Can't deliver it from you

You see all that He wants from us
Is just to praise His name
For us to understand the reason
Why He came

It was not just for a visit
To a relative or a friend
But to give us everlasting life
And to wash away all our sins

Like I always say
Before I write I pray to the sky
Because without My Father's love
O' for the grace of God go I

Terry Daniels

Sky Blue

Sky blue is something
That the whole world should see
A presence of love
For this whole world not just me

For us to acknowledge
A symbol from the Father
A miracle from the heavens
That could come from no other

For us to understand
That He is here for always
To be by your side
Throughout all of your days

To be on this earth
So that we could believe
An eternal life in His kingdom
Just ask to receive

From the beginning of time
He knew what would be real
A life that would live forever
That only his goodness could seal

To accept a beginning
That will have no end
To start a race
That only his true children will win

For you to know
That his food for thought
As He gave each one of us
A true path for us to walk

So please listen to your hearts
And feel as I do
Now look to the sun
And see Sky Blue

Live Or Memorex

Live or Memorex
Is this true or is it not
Is this a real cold?
Or is this just hot

Because everything you see
Is not a reality
So look in to your heart
And accept your mentality

Because what you think
It may not always be true
To know what is real
Only you can know you

See sometimes there may be things
That should be as it appears
With happiness or with sadness
They both could come with tears

Now this is the time
To understand right from wrong
As you close in on your journey
You must know where you will call home

Because these are the last days
And we are coming to the end
You must relinquish all your burdens
And ask for forgiveness for your sins

Because this is the time
That you must man up to your life
To get over your childish games
And to believe in the Lord Jesus Christ

You see your life is almost over
And your soul does need a rest
As you look at our Father's face
It will be all the way Live and no Memore

Terry Daniels

It's All Good

It's all good
Now what do you see
I welcome you to heaven
Now experience being free

Because now you are at home
Right where it begins
A paradise that is open
A place without sin

Everything is pure and clean
There is only one season
Freshness all around you
A brand new garden of Eden

Now you can see
There is nothing here that's fake
It's all here for your picking
It's right here for you to take

The days here are never cloudy
The night stays in bright
Compassion of love all around
That is here for your delight

I will be right here when you need me
I will always be by your side
This life that I promised you
Not once did I try to hide

Because I knew that it was hard
To believe in something you could not touch
To hear of a love so distant
Form a Soul that loved you so much

But like I said you are an image of Me
And now I will knock on wood
To hold you My precious child
Now it's all Good

When No One Is Looking

When no one is looking
What are you then?
Do you turn back to a one?
Or will you continue to be a ten

Because when no one's around
You can be your natural self
Will you be very poor?
Or flourished in great wealth

See the point that I am making
Do you know who you are?
Would you be a stand in?
Or would you be the star

See this is your life
And you should want to be the best that you can
But sometimes in life
We will all need a hand

You see this is a world
Where impurity is all around
But there is a lone that is with you
That will keep you on solid ground

It will always be there with you
It will never leave your side
No matter what your story is
There is nothing that you can hide

See no matter what you feel
No matter what you will do
There is a power here that is oh so great
That will always forever love you

See no matter what you are plotting
No matter what you are cooking
There are eyes on you no matter where you are
The Father's always looking

Terry Daniels

Work Out

Work out is something
That should give you strength
It should revive your body
It should also give you a hint

For you to understand
There is so much you should know
That there is more to life
And so much living to grow

To grow in a way
That your life must expand
From once a little boy
And now into a man

See this is the way
That your life should be
To understand change
Now to recognize Me

Me in this way
That I am the reason you exist
Of all of my creations
You are at the top of My list

For you to realize this
That you are second to none
The one love before you
That one love is My Son

For all to remember this
All your pains will be in your past
Now accept the love of the Father
Then rejoice in a life that will last

As you look around this world
These troubles that's all about
Give all your weighs to me
And accept My Eternal Work Out

Medication

Medication is something
That should give you relief
It should take away your pain
And stop all of your grief

See this is a condition
That will intensify your mind
Now open up your heart
And accept what you may find

Because if you need a drug
For any kind of reason
No matter what the month
No matter what the season

There must be something in your life
That is truly wrong
A structure in your body
A presence that doesn't belong

Because this is not the way
That your body was designed
It was built on true love
And peace of mind

See with any kind of aliment
There should be a cure
With an antidote so simple
And an answer so sure

You can go to any CVS
They will show you true dedication
But for your heart, mind, and soul
The Father is Your Medication

Terry Daniels

Yes I Am Blessed

Yes I am blessed
For all the things in my life
The troubles I have endured
All the pains and the strives

Because now I understand
That I am not alone
There is a place in my heart
That I can forever call home

It has always been there
But I did not see
I gave up all my burdens
And now at last I am free

Free that I finally realized
That this world is not forever
A change that occurred in my life
That can with stand and any kind of weather

See this was what I believed
And there could never be a change
I never knew of happy
My only thought was just pain

But this time I decided
That there must be another way
So I got down on my knees
And I decided to pray

As I finally did this thing
My whole world started to light
A switch came on inside
And I saw only bright

So with all of my heart and soul
I finally did confess
So I gave it all to My Father
Now I can say truly yes I Am Blessed

If Yesterday Was Today

If yesterday was today
There would be so much that I could see
To find out my true love
And that true love wasn't me

See you were always right there
Through my good times and my bad
You smiled with me when I was happy
You held me when I was sad

With each morning that I awake
Your soft body was always there
No matter what my feelings were
Your love you always shared

Because in your eyes my princess
I could do no wrong
To be my lady forever more
Not once was I alone

You stood right there with me
Through any and all of my situations
You were my heart and my soul
Without any hesitation

Whenever I would do something stupid
You would still be by my side
To pick up all of the pieces
And give me back my pride

You gave me a love so meaningful
That only you could truly give
Now without you my darling
There is no way that I can live

As one month passes another
And Father each second that I pray
I would do it all over
If Yesterday Was Today

Terry Daniels

An Angel On Earth

An angel on earth
How can this be true?
I have looked everywhere
And now I have finally found you

You see when you walked into my life
I could not describe how I felt
There is not a treasure on this world
That can compare to your wealth

A richness un-thought of
There is no money that could buy
Your true love that I long for
A blessing from the sky

Because I do not deserve
Someone so special and so free
To spend their entire life
Just loving only me

If you just give me this one chance
I promise you I would need no more
I will give you only happiness
And an everlasting life of joy

I will be there when you need me
And any desire that you wish
With all my hopes and promises
I will give my life for just one kiss

I will do anything that you ask
And I will never ever be late
I will be there when you call me
Without a second to hesitate

From the moment that I was created
And at the time of my birth
I knew that my dream lady was
An Angel on Earth

You Are Truly Special

You are truly special
And I have finally realized
You are much greater than any gift
And more valuable than any prize

You see before I met you
There were so many things I didn't know
Like where could I find true happiness
And a heart beat that really could show

A great thumping in my chest
A feeling I never had felt
A thing that would only occur
With the thought that you would have left

But that is only an experience
That I hope I will never go through
As I have given you all the possession of my heart
And an undying love for you

I will do anything for you
I would run any kind of a race
As long as each morning
I see your lovely face

Because everything about you
This I must truly learn
Whatever that would make you happy
Is my greatest concern

Because my day starts with you
With a sweet and gentle kiss
Anything afterwards
Is secondary on my last

When it is so cold and gloomy outside
In your arms I comfortly nestles
With my only thoughts on you yes
You are Truly Very Special

Terry Daniels

Desire

Desire
Is a lady
That her name does fit
She will give you a love
A love that will not lust

She will pour it all over you
Like a fresh summer shower
She will turn one of your seconds
Into an unforgettable hour

She will release your mind
And let your soul run free
She will reveal her perfect body
For only your eyes to see

She will introduce you to a passion
That you never seen or heard
She will present to you a lust
Without even saying a word

She will give you new thoughts
That would have never crossed your minds
She will put you in a state of shock
Until she says it's time

She will set up a standard
No matter how much you reach it's not enough
She will program your mind
That all it wants is one touch

She will make you feel like
That you are walking on air
She will express to your heart
Only her love you must share

She will unchain that volcano
That will ignite all of your fire
When you meet this true woman
Then you would have found Desire

What Can I Say

What can I say
Everything that I have asked
You have delivered
Without even a second thought
Of the word reconsidered

So what can I do?
And now I understand
That You are for real
And this is Your Plan

You see Father I have tried
To do things on my own
But the results on that thought
Always leaves me all alone

I am so tired of being unhappy
I am tired of being hurt
So now I have decided
To turn to what really does work

Because all of my life
I've always known that You were there
To be with me through my heart aches
To show me that You care

What would I have done
Without the love that you have given
At anytime You could have chose
To stop that life I was living

But You continued to stay with me
Through all the troubles that I was involved
For me to think that I was getting over
All of those things You resolved

Now My Son as you speak to Me
The only thing You must do is just pray
Now just trust and believe in Me
There is no more For You to Say

Terry Daniels

I'm Still Standing

I'm still standing
How can this be?
I gave my life to Jesus
And it feels so good being free

Lord how can I thank you
For all that you have done
My race was long and very rough
But with You I have finally won

I feel so good inside
That there is nothing that I won't do
To show everything and everybody
How much I do love You

You have been there for me
Time after time, after time
When I thought I could not go on
You always showed me a sign

A path that you directed for me
A course that I must stay
But anytime I have had second thoughts
All I had to do was just pray

But as I have grown older
It was really not that hard
All I had to do
Was keep faith in my God

Now matter what you may do
He will never take away His love
His purpose and His goal is
An everlasting life above

As I look back on my life
I felt that it was so demanding
So when I turned it all over to My Father
Only by His grace that I'm still standing

Drama

Drama
Is a word
That is much bigger than it is spelled
To have drama in your life
You must be able to sell

Because this thing is all about you
And there is no one else that matter
For you to accept all the glory
And is responsible for all of the flatter

You can take one simple thing
And turn it into what you need
Like you could blow up any conversation
Just by planting the seed

So no matter what it will be
Or what it will not
As long as the outcome
Is everything you wanted you got

Because if you are not the center of attraction
This thing should not take place
Anything of great importance
Only then should you show your face

You see this is not the way
That this world was designed
It was built on love and happiness
And peace of mind

For all of us to understand
That there is only one true love you should know
A Father that looks over us
As He watches us below

As I think of our Lord Jesus Christ
When He walked through this world with honor
The only thing that He showed was love
And there was no drama

Terry Daniels

My Mother

My mother is a lady
That there are no words to describe
A true love that is real
A true love that is alive

As I look at her and wonder
About all of the things that I see
And to know and understand
That her true love is really me

The many things that I have done
All the promises that I have made
But there is one thing that I am a sure of
That her love will never fade

I have hurt her so many times
But she is always right there
To forgive all my wrongs
And to show that she care

You see there are questions that are asked
And no answers to receive
But there is a voice inside all of us
All you must do is believe

Because The Father that I'm speaking of
He knows all of our thoughts
A journey that was given to you
A path that you must walk

A life so easy
That we will see each day
A direction so clear
All you have to do is just pray

To give you a life
That could come from no other
To direct you to him
He gave us our Mother

Why Do They Persecute Me

Why do they persecute me?
What have I done?
I came for one reason
I came as His son

To show this world
The reason that you exist
All the things that has been created
You are on the top of the list

Because you are the image
Of whom we really are
We are right here with you
No matter how near or far

Now please understand My curiosity
Because you are the reason I care
All the pain, heartaches, and troubles
Remember I also share

Because anything on earth that happens
It is already in our sight
So please don't try to hide the wrong
Just come to me I'll make it right

But for me to sit here and wonder
What else I can do
I will die so that you can live again
Just to show My love is true

Now what else do you want
Just please give me a hint
For Me and My Father will both know
The reason that I was sent

But now as I hang from the cross
For all of Our Children sins are free
But for Me to think of all the love that I have shown
And I wonder why they still Persecute Me

Terry Daniels

To Be Disappointed

To be disappointed
Is such a bad feeling
Something that really hurts
And so very revealing

A thing that's inside of you
That you may try to hide
An emotion so troublesome
That you cannot deny

Because it will be there
No matter where you may go
It will not leave you

And your face will definitely show

So what must you do
To get over the anger and frustration
To take it all away
To solve that equation

You see when problems like these arrives
And you think there's no way to turn
Please listen to me very careful
And accept what I have learned

You see life could change
Like a breath of air
One moment everyone loves you
The next one no one cares

But you always must remember
Whatever your situations
There is a love right there with you
Without any hesitation

So when you feel this way
You must turn to the one who is anointed
He is always right there with you
Even more when you are Disappointed

You Made My Day

You made my day
So I can see
This journey that I am on
That will set Me free

Free from everything
On this earth that exist
Freedom from all those burdens
And never ending list

But no matter what will develop
Between now and then
There is one thing you can be sure of
That there will always be sin

Because it is here
And it is here to stay
There is only one solution
And it is so simple just pray

You see you cannot control
Everything that is around you
It will be your decision
On what you desire to choose

Because this is a world
That has both love and hate
Either one of these things
You could easily relate

You see now is the final time
That you make your life's stand
Our Savior is waiting for you
He's reaching out His hand

As He stands right by you
To show you the correct way
Then he welcomes you his Kingdom
He smiles and says you Made My Day

Terry Daniels

The Last Ride

The last ride to me means
That the thrill is gone
Where your earthly body
Should know where its home

Because when this time happens
And trust me it will
There is a hole in the ground
And it will be filled

Because back to the earth
That our bodies will return
Plaques placed on your grave
For all of those who are concerned

A memory that you will leave
For everyone can see
But some will not understand
That at last you are free

Free from a life
That carries so much pain
Free from a world
That will continue to rain

But this was the life
That you have left behind
Now if you followed your birth path
Then Heaven you will find

Because our Father has been waiting
And he has been waiting so long
To greet you His Child
And to welcome you back home

You see this was a hard journey
With the Lord Jesus staying by your side
He will welcome you to Paradise
And that was The Last Ride

What Shall I Do

What shall I do?
I am so lost and depressed
What shall I do?
My body needs a rest

I am tired and I am weary
And I feel so all alone
My world has collapsed
My mind wants to roam

Too far away places
Where I can be safe and warm
Away from everything
Away from any harm

I need a structure to depend on
And I need it right now
I want to ask questions
And I don't know who or how

Well My Child please listen
I am always here for you
My love is always present
Now just look for something blue

Far above the clouds
Away from all the stars
And ever loving relationship
A whisper from a far

You see I will never leave you
Because these times I am at my best
See I am Your Father
And I am the only one that can give you rest

So trust and believe me
Please remember what is true
When your burdens seems so over whelming
Just turn them over to me that's what You Shall Do

Forever More

Forever more
Is the phrase that I will speak
Now my beautiful angel
Only you must believe

Because you are the one
That I have chosen for life
My love, my baby, my honey
I must see you each night

I know this is rather sudden
And it hasn't been very long
But for you my special lady
It's time for you to come home

To be there each morning
Of each day, of each week
All my prayers have been answered
All my stars have been reached

A journey that we will travel
A new world we will see
A love so everlasting
Forever you and me

Because anything in your past
I really don't need to know
Because you are my lady now
And that's all, you must show

You see now it is us
You and I together
To take on any challenges
And endure all the weathers

Now understand this, my lady
There's not enough love that I could pour
Because with each beat of my heart
Says I will Love You Forever More

My First And My Last

My first and my last
This is what I see
Is this for real
Is this for me?

For all of my life I have waited
For this special time
For my true love to come to me
And I know that she is mine

From the first day that I was born
And placed on this earth
To find you my precious lady
For eternity I will search

No matter how far away
No matter how long
I will never ever give up on you
Until my search brings you home

To my paradise to stay
To keep you safe and warm
For me to love and hold you gently
To keep you from any harm

Because I will be right by your side
And I will never ever leave
For us to take our marriage vows
And to plant our seeds

To symbolize our place in heaven
That only our Father could give
To show our children so they can understand
This is the true way to live

See when destiny comes into your life
It may come quick and fast
But when it showed me my soul mate
She will be My First and My Last

Terry Daniels

Honey I Do

Honey I do
Anything that you may ask
Honey I will forever
Take on any kind of task

Because you are the only one
That can turn my life around
A diamond in the rough
That I am so glad that I found

To dream of someone special
That you know you don't deserve
With the smile on her face
And you don't have to say a word

The twinkle in your eyes
The expression on your face
Tells me ever so gentle
That you have me in a very special place

A place that is unspoken
That you have let very few people see
A paradise uncharted
An island of tranquility

A sweet smell of jasmine
The soft whisper of the wind
The love that's in my heart
A combination that will blend

Because now I am so happy
And there are no words that I can describe
A blessing from the heavens
A love that will never die

As you speak to me so gently
And baby I know this is true
With all of the passions of this whole world
I will politely say Honey I Do

Teach Me

Teach me the things
That I should know
To show me the way
That your eyes should glow

Glowing in a way
That should make me feel
That this love is possible
And could be real

But for me to feel
So deep in my mind
The total perfect woman
A true love that I can find

But to look at you
And for you to smile
I am only 22
And I feel like a child

In a way a lady so perfect
A lady so fine
A woman so beautiful
Could never be mine

To look and to see
There are angels on earth
No gold no treasures
Could ever touch her worth

Then I am back
Just where I started
Depressed and upset
And very broken hearted

But the love in my heart
It must be set free
So please my dream lady
Will you please Teach Me?

Terry Daniels

My Wife

My wife is a lady
That I love oh so much
With each second I am away from her
I long for her loving touch

Because she is the breath of fresh air
That I must see each day
I prayed to my Father above
To send her my way

No matter what I think
No matter what I may do
The only love in my world
Will forever belong to you

To stay with me forever
Through thick and through thin
For her everlasting love
This I must truly win

As I see her with our children
All the wisdom that she shows
The love that she gives to them
Only the love a mother knows

Sometimes there will be problems
Where we both don't agree
And then I would sit back and think
Then I find out the problems was me

She understands so very well
That sometimes she must stand alone
She is also very aware
That a house does not make a home

As I wake up each morning
And for the rest of my life
The best part of me will
Forever be My Wife

Welcome To My World

Welcome to my world
Now you will finally get to see
This will be our home
Now at last you are free

Free from a life
That you thought would last
Free from everything
Free from even your past

You see I knew and understood
What this would really cost
So I gave you My only Son
So that you would not get lost

You see this was oh so hard
And it hurts Me so much
To show this to all of My Children
How much I wanted their special touch

For me to know and believe
That this creation was no mistake
To give You My Own Blood
And not to even hesitate

For Me to know and understand
That this is exactly what I desire
Now please give it to your soul
And there will be no fire

Because this is what I wanted
For you to be here right by My side
To show you My little angels
A true love I will never deny

So as I give you all of My love
There are no diamonds or pearls
That could even scratch the surface of you
So welcome to My Word

Terry Daniels

Now It Is Over

Now it is over
It is finally all done
This mission that We started
This mission that We won

Because this world is in turmoil
And there is no other way out
To change this situation
There must be a complete turn about

Because this is the world
That My Father loves so much
With each shred of life
It came from His loving touch

Everything that moves
Everything that walks
Everything that listens
Everything that talks

The trees, the grass, and the flowers
The birds as they fly
The sun and the moon and the stars
All in this big blue sky

Everything you have seen
Everything you have heard
It was all given to you
With a whisper of his word

This new love that He has given you
A brand new life to start
A place in His heaven
A great love in His heart

You see all of your problems are gone
There's no more looking over your shoulders
As I return My Soul to My Father
Now it is all Over

So Far But Yet So Close

So far but yet so close
Something so distant that you must believe
A vision in front of you
That only your soul can see

To except a miracle
That has not come to pass
A thought that you have waited for
A dream that will last

Something that you have prayed for
And have waited for so long
A desire in your life
That will take you back home

To a place where everything started
And that there will be no end
A love so pure and simple
A world without sin

Now could you just imagine?
Something so clean and so true
Something with one mission
And it is to love only you

Because with each day that starts
There is a new journey to explore
A thing that will confront you
Like a house with closed doors

As you take each step
There will be something you have never seen
The closer that you get
Then you wonder what does it mean?

You see this is what your life is about
Would you prefer a cactus or a rose?
Now think of the love that you have shown our Father
Is He so Far away or is He so Close

I Can Do That

I can do that
Anything that I choose
I can make you win
Or I can make you lose

I can make you happy
Or I can make you frown
I can turn your whole life
Completely upside down

You see that is not my purpose
Nor is it my reason
This is not the time of year
Nor is it the season

Because this is not the love
That I promised I would give
I gave you a life of hope and freedom
And a choice to live

Because whatever you decide
It will always be up to you
I gave it to this whole wide world
Not only just a few

You see this would be your life's decision
Will you succeed or will you fail
Will you see My heaven?
Or will you just go to hell

See all of these things that you know
Are completely all up to you
Whatever your decisions will be
My love will forever be true

But for Me to tell you right from wrong
And My child this is a fact
For Me to make you do anything
I Cannot Do That

There Is Something Wrong With This Picture

There is something wrong with this picture
What don't you see?
I'm living in this world
A world without Thee

So how can I live this way?
I don't understand
This is a great worry
And this is not my plan

Because my days seems like nights
And my nights seems like my days
Everything is all so wrong
In every kind of way

I see no future now
I don't know of the past
I don't understand happiness
I wonder will this last

I worry about everything
And there is nothing that I can change
My mind is so confused
I feel like I am deranged

So what can I do
With all these problems I need solved
I would ask my friends
But they don't want to get involved

My life is in turmoil
And I see it's coming to an end
I have no defense
This battle I can't win

As I understand my situation
I begin to pray for a fixture
This thing was right in my face
My Father was not in my picture

Terry Daniels

I Want To Be Rich

I want to be rich
Then what would I do
I would buy everything
I would buy it brand new

Because with that kind of cash
I would not take anything used
Nothing that's not clean
Nothing that's been abused

You see this would be my world
And everything would be real
I would pay just what it cost
I would not haggle for a deal

Because I would have the money
To buy whatever I would choose
No matter if it is over priced
I would not care if I lose

Because this is my vision of a dream
And nothing in it is right
Because the world that I live in
Is as different as day is to night

Now let us look at this real world
Because it is not the way that it should be
Living a life where there is death and destruction
And without the love of Thee

Because He made a promise to us all
A world of milk and honey
To give you all the things that you need
In a paradise without any money

No matter what your occupations is
You might even be digging a ditch
But as long as you have Jesus Christ
In your life my friend You Are Rich

Each Morning That I Wake

Each morning that I wake
What do I see?
Something I never knew of
How to be free

To not have any worries
No struggles or no pains
To finally expect the sunshine
And a very small chance rain

You see I am finally relaxed
Now I take each day as it comes
As I accept in my heart
That my Father's work has been done

Because this was his vision
And only he understood
A finale to it all
Like only he truly could

You see sometimes you may reach
For stars that are out of your sight
You may think its day time
But really it's at night

You see hopes are only hopes
And this is oh so true
But no matter what that outcome is
Remember that the Father will forever love you

So please understand this, my friend
Rather there is a win or a loss
He will always stand with you
Because that is in his clause

So as I think of my life
And I truly know what's at stake
I know that he is with me
Each Morning That I Wake

Terry Daniels

Kicked Into Heaven

Kicked into heaven
What does this mean?
Something unlikely
Something unseen

Because this thing did happen
And it is so true
This thing that could happen
And it could happen to you

As I look at the Father's creation
This world is so gone
Everything that I thought was good
Right now it is all wrong

To party one day
And then the next
Having so much fun
I felt like I was blessed

Because everything I want to do
It will be free for the asking
When you get tired of that one place
All you had to do is start packing

But one day I got sick
And I had lost so much weight
But then out of the clear blue
I asked the Father for my soul to take

But then something happened
And it felt oh so great
The tears ran from my eyes
I asked my Father, am I too late?

Now as this revolution unfolded
It was about a quarter till eleven
The devil heard me crying for my Father
He became so mad that He Kicked Me Into Heaven

How Low Can I Go

How low can I go?
This was not my plan
Looking up at the ground
Where right now I stand

I can't see the top
Of nothing that I should believe
Not one thing is good
Only the bottom of the sea

As I look into the mirror
And what did I discover
A person with no ambitions
No life to recover

So what can I say
I feel nothing inside
I don't have any hope
I've lost all of my pride

But one day I woke up
And had this unusual vision
So I said to myself
I must finally make a decision

Of which way to go
What path will I choose?
There is only one that is left
And that one I cannot lose

Because these problems that I have
Are not for only me to share
A love one that stays with me
A true friend that really does care

To not have acknowledge my Father
As he looks down at me below
I will turn my life over to my Jesus
Now I wonder how High Will I Go

Terry Daniels

Umbrella

Umbrella to me
Means protection from all the pains
It should keep you dry and warm
From any kind of rain

You see there could be something in your life
That will bring troubles and despair
But this umbrella that I speak of
It will be with you it will share

Because this is a world
That no one should be by themselves
See one is so lonely
And it carries no help

You see things will happen
And they won't be a part of your plan
Now without a friend to lean on
Alone you must stand

But there is something that is with you
That will see you face to face
A love that will surround you
That created this human race

Because this is what love is
So easy and so pure
He will always give it to you
And you can rest assured

You see now it's time to study
Because this may be your last test
To accept what the world offers
Or to be heavenly blessed

You see you can be afraid and scared
And you could hide in a cellar
Or you can give your life to the Father
And live happily under His Umbrella

God Don't Like Ugly

God don't like ugly
Then how do you know
Just look into the mirror
And your expression will show

Because anything you don't know
You should always ask
That is the first step
Of taking on any task

Because if you are not sure
Of everything that you do
Then you must look deep into your heart
And then know that it's true

You see the first impression of anything
Is what you will remember
Even if it's in January
Or even if it's in December

Because things that you see
May not always be what they appear
Because if it's not 100 percent
Then it is not all the way clear

You see the point I'm trying to make
Is as different as day is to night
To love this lost world
Or to believe that your paradise is in sight

You see I know of something that's real
As your life will come and will go
I know of a forever love
That is looking over us below

I know of a place where you can live
Safe warm and snuggly
A heaven flourished in only beauty
Because God Don't Like Ugly

Terry Daniels

Something Is Wrong

Something is wrong
And I don't understand
Why is this happening
This is not my plan

It seems like I am stuck
Between time and space
A weird feeling inside of me
And it can't be erased

You see I don't know
Rather I'm coming or going
And the worst thing about it
How would I react by knowing

It just seems that I am lost
And there is no way I can get out
I am trapped inside my body
And I am trying to shout

But no one can hear me
And there is nothing I can do
So with all of my inner strength
I'm crying out to You

You see this is something
That no one in this world can do
So right now at this time
I turn my soul over to You

So help me my Father
I'm tired and I want to come home
I cannot enjoy happy here
So that means Something Is Wrong

Snapshot

Snapshot is something
That you will take right then
It could be a loss
Or it could be a win

Because the desires that you achieve
Must come from deep within your heart
A purpose in your life
Only you will know the start

You see this is no joke
And this is about you
Every step that you take
Each one must be true

You see mistake will be made
And troubles will arise
But at the end of your journey
Your determination will be your prize

Because you would have given your all
And nothing but the best you will accept
The pains that only you know
The many tears that you had wept

To achieve any goal
There is much more than meets the eye
Anytime you may have doubts
There is always the blue sky

So now you must buckle down
And there is no way that you can stop
There is so much depending on you
And it is much greater than a Snapshot

Terry Daniels

My Dream Girl

My dream girl
What do I see?
The total package of love
Designed only for me

Everything about you
All of my desires
Any of my hopes
I could not reach no higher

To think of you so much
There is not a word that I can say
All the feelings in my heart
As they grow stronger each day

These passions that I have found
That was buried within
Any hurt that I've been through
My broken heart you have mend

When you entered into my life
I thought this would be a test
As you took control of my mind
I knew then I was blessed

For me to relinquish
Any pains from my past
As you unlocked my closed door
And showed a future that would last

To see you as I see you
And to feel as I do
To know and to believe
That your love forever true

Now for me to understand
There is not a greater gift in this world
As I hold you oh so gently
And to know that you are My Dream Girl

Ms. Lady

Ms. Lady, Ms. Lady
Where can I find you?
I've looked everywhere
And I still don't have a clue

I have looked all around
I have looked near and far
I have even looked to the sky
And have even counted every star

Your presence is needed desperately
Because there are things that needs to be done
My world starts only with you
You are my bright and shining sun

The moments that I am away from you
I'm so lonely and very depressed
With each thought in my mind
Your soft body I am longing to caress

My future will always be with you
Forever and this I will truly say
There is an undying love in my heart
That will grow stronger each and every day

You see without you my princess
My life I will live alone
Because of the thought of you not in my world
My heart will turn in to stone

Because you are the only cure my friend
To all of my disappointments and frustrations
I want just one perfect love
And it would be you in an eternal relation

Because with everything that I desire in life
And this one time it won't be hazy
With all of my love and my heart
I give it all to you Ms. Lady

Terry Daniels

Marriage

Marriage to me
What does it mean?
To find that perfect person
Then to live your life's dream

To stay with someone forever
No matter all the troubles or drama
To be by there side always
To love, trust and to honor

You see everything is open
And there are no closed doors
A friendship with each other
A new world to explore

You see when this commitment was made
It was given from the heart
A life that will live for infinity
A brand new beginning to start

As you give your mind
Your body and soul
To do our Father's will
And to follow our Father's role

Because this is the reason
That He brought two souls together
To stay by each other's side
Through all storms and weathers

You see this is for real
And there is no way it can be changed
This is our Father's thought
And there is no other way it could be arranged

As your children are born into this world
In this Christian heritage
There is a star in the sky
That will symbolize your Marriage

Pretty Girl

Pretty girl
Is a lady that enough
Has not been said
Each second spent with her
Is a new chapter to be read

Because every time I am with her
There is something else that is new
A change all about her
Another thing to review

I do not know why
Nor will I try to understand
I will give her all that I have
Just to be her only man

There is not a day that passes
There is not a dream that I will not sleep
There is not a moment of any hour
That she doesn't make my life complete

I will spend my whole life
Just thinking how to please
Hoping and praying
For her heart to be released

Because whenever she offers it
There will be no turning back
I will cling to her forever
And that is a true fact

My world would revolve around her
And she will be the center of it all
The shield that protected me
Just one kiss destroyed that wall

I will be your protector
I would give you the world
I will love you for eternity My Pretty Girl

Terry Daniels

Wedding Anniversary

Wedding anniversary
Today is the day
That our Father has brought us together
In a very special way

For us to share a life
For always just you and I
To consent to a love
That came from the sky

For all of my life
I have been waiting for you
To understand a happiness
And to know that it is true

Because every time I see you
My heart skips a beat
To know that you are the only one
That can truly set it free

There have been times that I felt
That I would be all alone
No one to care for
No one to call my own

But then one day I heard your voice
And my whole life started to change
The sun became oh so bright
And for once I saw no rain

Now every since that moment
My world has went in reverse
All the time I thought I was happy
Now I know I was only hurt

You see now is the time
To start on the nursery
Because these special times with you my love
Forever will be our Wedding Anniversary

Are You Ready

Are you ready
For what's going to happen
If not too bad
If so start clapping

Because this is the time
That we all have been waiting for
Every life is revealed
No more closed doors

The life that you lived
Will soon be shown
All the skeletons in your closet
Will soon be known

Because this is the day
That there will be no more lies
All your questions, answered
All from the big blue sky

You see this was the reason
That you were here
So if you know of the Father
Then you should have no fear

I don't understand
Please make me see
To accept what the world had
Or to believe in Thee

These things on earth
They look like so much fun
You forgot about your reason here
You forgot the race you should have won

You see my friend
You must continue to stay steady
Because the time is oh so close
So Are You Ready

Terry Daniels

It's A Good Thing

It's a good thing
And that I do know
My journey will be over soon
Then I will understand my role

Father you promised
That this was only the beginning
No more physical pain
My soul would start mending

It took a very long time
For me to recognize
That this world is an illusion
And Heaven is my prize

Father as I sit here
I cannot even imagine
Your paradise oh so close
Right over the horizon

To a place we all have heard of
And everyone should see
A one way trip to eternity
No cost just free

Now please listen very closely
And try to understand
Could you have given up your life
To save any man

You see this is a question
That we may never know why
Like I said before there's only one place
The great blue sky

To finally get here
Where the glorious angels sings
And happiness is everywhere
Then to see The Father now
It's A Good Thing

I'm Coming

I'm coming and there's nothing
That can be done about it
I begged, I pleaded
I even shout it

For this day was told
Time after time again
I asked only one simple thing
To relinquish all of your sins

A burden that was bestowed on you
From day one
How do I know?
Because I am My Father's Son

The things that I endured
Were only a small part
For everyone to believe
The true love in Our Hearts

You see you all must understand
That there was a part of Us that We gave
For you all to live for eternity
Just ask to be saved

You see the doors has always been open
And they will never ever be closed
For the evil that you inherited
Was the reason why I rose

So no matter the times that you think
Your life is not worth living
Just call on Us
And we will explain what We are giving

You see this is the day
That there will be no more running
Because this is the end
And yes I'm Coming

Slow Rolling

Slow rolling
What does this mean?
Just taking your time
And living your dream

Because this is your life
Now it's time to be real
Now understand what you want
And accept how you feel

Because this will be a voyage
That you will experience it alone
A place where it will separate
All your rights from your wrongs

You see we all have a destination
That we all should fulfill
A life that came with you
That desire and the will

You see the things you decide
And things you will do
Just remember one thing
That Our Father loves you

Because we are the reason
Why Our Jesus did come
To give us eternal life
For His will would be done

As I look at this world
And all the dangers that is unfolding
It's time to turn to Jesus Christ
Your soul is now in jeopardy so there is no more time for
Slow Rolling

I Wonder

I wonder what it will be like
When I finally meet You
Everything that I have read, everything I saw
Will they all be true?

How did You get this power?
Where did it come from?
I know about You
I heard about Your Son

There is so much to ask
And I don't know where to start
But every time I think of You
A strange feeling enters my heart

It's just like a flutter
That runs all over me
A sensation so unusual
A feeling of totally free

It's like there's nothing around
That can give me any fear
Just that one little simple thought
That's knowing that You are here

I know that my soul
That You value so much
I could not be me
Without Your special touch

Because there is no way
That this world would exist
Everything that You have created
You sealed it with Your kiss

The trees that grows oh so high
The roaring of the thunder
Everything that lives My Father
No more Will I Wonder

Terry Daniels

Front Street

Front street to me means
Right then and right there
No matter the location
It could be anywhere

Because in any situations
Sometimes there are things you don't know
Because anything you can't see
Eventually it will show

See you can run into a problem
That you may think its wrong but it's right
The results on that event
Could result into a fight

Because you put your nose
Where it did not belong
Like most things like that
It always ends up in such a sad song

But what I am trying to tell you
You can accept this or not
Because this is your life
You better remember what you were taught

I'm going to tell you this
And you can take it as you please
Your soul is headed for hell
So you better start getting on your knees

You see the time is now
And you can't wait until tomorrow
Your pain starts right here
And your suffering will soon follow

So remember what I said
And please tell everyone that you meet
Our father is coming very soon
Now you are on Front Street

It's Time To Bounce

It's time to bounce
Love don't live here anymore
This journey is over
It's time for another door

Because the next step to you take
Will be a new experience
A place you might like
That you would need a new clearance

Because everything is different
It's a brand new thing to learn
Something that is unusual
Another thought for concern

Because this is the time to settle down
And figure out where you stand
Because every time you make a move
You really should have a plan

Now feel what I am saying
And please take this to heart
There is a world out there that's cruel and cold
Now Heaven is the place to start

To begin at the top
There is not a better place to be
To ask for the vision
That only Our Father can see

Because this thought that He had
From the beginning of all time
A home that will last forever
A peace that you will find

Now please understand this
And this is the only time it will be announced
A life that will live for eternity
Now do you still think
It's Time To Bounce

Terry Daniels

I Belong to You

I belong to you
Finally I will do this
With all that I am
There will be no more lists

Because everything that I am about
I put it all in Your hands
Because I know in my heart
That I am the reason of Your plan

I thank you for all of the things
That you have done for me in my life
Whenever I would lose my faith
Your love was always insight

You stayed right there by my side
You never left me alone
I know that You will be with me
Until You bring me home

I cannot wait for the day
That I meet You face to face
Then my soul would truly know
That I finally won my race

To see all of your glory above
And to experience a life without sin
To truly understand my life
And the reason You chose to defend

You see Father I am only human
And there are so many things I don't know
All I had to do was so simple
And Your glory really did show

But now as I live my life
And I know that my days are few
So with the last breath that I take
Now I Belong To You

Junk In The Trunk

Junk in the trunk
How did it get there?
It came so very quick
And I don't even know where

But this is something
That it must get gone
Because in my house
That junk does not belong

Because I can choose what ever
And decide what I need
Because I took everything
Just to fulfill my greed

But why would you take
Things of no concern
A pattern you have developed
A poison you have learned

But this is your life
And you must accept what you receive
And trust right in your face
That all you have to do is believe

Because this world is coming
And it's coming to the end
So for your own sake
You better start looking at your sins

Because the time is coming now
And this world will be gone
So these last few days
You better decide which place will be home

Now think of this reality
Why the ark never sunk
For Our Father to clean up this world
He had to get rid of the Junk In The Trunk

Terry Daniels

You Done Lost Your Mind

You done lost your mind
Now what do you mean
Something that you think is real
It may not be what it seems

You see false is always false
There is no other way to think
Because if it's not a float
Then it will truly sink

You see sometimes there are things in life
That you don't know how to get
You see everyone would like to be a star
But they will not sacrifice for that success

Now understand this thought
What are your desires?
Would you like to go for the gusto?
Or are you just the town crier

You see either one you pick
It will be your choice to choose
Because anytime you gamble with your life
There is always a possibility to lose

Now please listen to the reason
Because there is only one thing that's sure
A life that you could live for eternity
A love that is forever pure

Now trust and believe this my friend
And this is not a lie
No matter what all your troubles are
Just pass them on to the sky

Now this is for real and it's up to you to start trusting
Because you are running out of time
Because if you don't know of the love of Our Father
Then you Done Lost Your Mind

Show And Tell

Show and tell
What does this do
To know that you are right
This thing that you will prove

Because if you don't believe in yourself
Now who else will
Too have someone doubt you
Can you imagine how that feels

To trust in your heart
And to know that you can
To see what your future holds
And to follow your plans

Because this is your baby
And your passion is very true
No one knows this love
No one but only you

Now just sit back and think
And relax your entire mind
To start up any happiness
There's one place you must find

You see Our Father is true
And Our Father does care
To start any adventure
The Father should also share

You see the Father is the one
Who knew you from birth
He knows of your short coming
He knows of your worth

Because this is a world
That knows the Heaven and the Hell
So whichever one that you choose
It will be your Show And Tell

Terry Daniels

One, On, One

One, On, One
Means you and me
As I look at my life
It's the only way to be free

Free from every thing
And a better way to live
To find a better life
That only You can live

As I look all around
Things do change every day
For me to understand
That there is, only one way

Each morning that I'm here
I find someone has left this Earth
At the end of each journey
They will know their value and worth

Because everyone here
Was given a choice
For at the end of your voyage
They will hear only one voice

Then you will understand
The road that you have paved
Will it lead you to Hell?
Or will you be saved

You see this is something
That no one knows of deliverance
A part of our lives
That no one has experienced

So as I get older
I feel my life is almost done
So I cannot wait to meet you, My Father
This time… One on One

I Want More

I want more
Than what do see
I want more
Because I hold this key

For me to expect
Better things in my life
To reach all of my goals
And to accept any sacrifice

Because challenges are made
For people with desires
Each time you get close to one
You must raise the bar higher

Because as I look at my life
I will never reach the top
The drive in my heart
Will never say stop

Before I finish one thing
I must start on another
Another challenge to seek
Another voyage to discover

I don't know when
How, what, or why
But the ambitions in my soul
Does come from the sky

A sky so glorious
Beautiful and blue
As I listens to its voice
It says, "My child I love you"

As I think of my Father
All His love He has poured
Even though it's a lot
Still I Want More

Terry Daniels

Survival

Survival means to me
Whatever it takes you will do
Because this is your life
And it's all about you

Because you command
Your future and desires
Do you want to stay where you are?
Or will you reach higher

Now think about what you can do
No matter who says no
Everyone should have a dream
At the end of their rainbow

You see sometimes in life
You may think that you are alone
No one to turn to
No place to call home

But there is someone who loves you
And all your burdens they will share
A shoulder you can lean on
A love that really cares

From the time the you were born
You had a life that came with a plan
A relationship that has no boundaries
A love that came from no man

You see whenever you need answers
And there is only one place that is real
Just look deep into your soul
Then our Father you will feel

Now just think of your family
Each home should have a Bible
With the Father's Book on life
It will help you with Survival

Done Deal

Done deal to me means
Over with no more
End of the journey
No more boundaries, no more shores

To start this thing
From the beginning till the end
To cross that finish line
And to know how to win

Because everyone does not have
That fire to achieve
If it is not working for them
Most likely they will leave

Please understand this
It was given to you at birth
To know of your true quality
Your value and your worth

You see this is a world
That was built out of truth and faith
Guided and directed by the Son and Father
Without any delay

Assuring you a paradise
That only His righteous children to share
Delivering a loving home
Without a doubt they do care

To be given something for nothing
What a wonderful thought
Something so priceless
A love that can't be bought

As the Father looked all around
Only the darkness was real
After all His work was over
He looked to His Son and said Done Deal

Terry Daniels

Do You Remember Your Past

Do you remember your past?
How can you forget?
A life that you lived
About some things you regret

Because it will be there
And it will never go away
This thing that you know
Inside of you it will stay

A problem that lingers
That's all ways on your mind
A burden that won't leave
It's with you all the time

The problem that is on my mind
It is slowly escalating
The toe holds that I held on my life
It is slowly, slowly fading

You see this is not the reason
Of the way my life should be
My world should be open
My heart totally free

The burdens that I carry
They are not for me to keep
I need a total change over
A peace for me to seek

But where do I turn
What shall I do?
The only choice that is in my life
Is to turn it all over to You

You see my Father I need You
I need a true love that will last
So please my Lord help me
To get over all of My Past

Resentment

Resentment
What does it really mean?
Something you do not like
Or that is what it seems

Because there are things in life
That will get under your skin
An irritating feeling
A poison that is within

Something that you despise
A trouble on your mind
Something that you must get rid of
A relief you must find

But how do you know
Where do you search?
Anyway – out
Anything that will work

Because it is a pest
That you don't want it around
Something that's no good
An unhappy you have found

But this is a life
That has both good and bad
Some things make you happy
While others makes you sad

But no matter what the situation
There is always a place you can go
Whenever you feel down and out
There is a rainbow that will always show

So whatever may be the problem
There is a love that will show contentment
Just release all of your worries
And let Him deal with your Resentment

Terry Daniels

Who Would Ever Thunk It?

Who would ever thunk it?
As I stand here and think to myself
There is a life before me
That has such great wealth

I am not speaking
Of diamonds and emeralds
I am talking of a promise made
As I look at this beautiful symbol

This rainbow that I am speaking
It has such beautiful colors and designs
It will remind you of a love
That is so easy to find

You see whenever you get lonely
And filled with concerns
There is always someone who will listen
And a place to turn

Because they know your thoughts
Your heart aches and pains
They would know when the sun would shine
And even more when it rains

But how does it feel
To know someone that knows you
Better than you know yourself?
It may sound strange but it is so true

True as this life
That you were given to live
True as a love
That only they could give

As I look over my life
Sometimes I wish I could just junk it
But for me to know that someone really loves me
Who would ever Thunk It?

Stuck On Stupid

Stuck on stupid
Why haven't you learned?
Each direction that you choose
Is always the same turn

Because if you do the same thing
Over and over again
The results that you will get
It will be a loss and never a win

So why do you do it?
Now is the time to stop
You will continue to be at the bottom
And you will never reach the top

But there is a way
That you can change it all around
To find a new direction
A new hope to be found

You see whenever that your vision
Is not clear at all
There is a navigator all around
That is waiting for your call

He will be there through your storms
He will be with you through any weather
He will protect and hold you
He will make everything much better

Whenever you feel lost
And you don't know where to go
Just ask Him for guidance
He will show you your rainbow

Just like an arrow
That you may think came from cupid
Now give it all to Jesus Christ
He will change all of your thoughts on Stuck On Stupid

Terry Daniels

Don't Hate Me

Don't hate me
Because I did all I could
I gave You all of My love
Like I promised I would

To show you a life
That no one else could have done
I gave you all I have
I gave you my only Son

For you to understand
And for you to truly realize
That I am your salvation
And I am your prize

To give you a life
That will never have an end
To live for eternity
A promise I will defend

You see this was the only reason
That I gave you My heir
So that you could believe that I loved you
And that you would know that I cared

You see this was a decision
That I had to make sure that it was clear
So just trust and believe in Me
And I will promise you no fear

Because I am the truth
And I am the light
I will protect and cherish you
With all of My might

As I created you my child
I gave you an eternal life to be free
Just trust in My word and Don't Hate Me

Jealousy

Jealousy to me is the root
To all of earth's problems
Even if you had everything
That still wouldn't be able to solve them

Because as you receive one thing
You are also looking at another
No matter what your thought would be
It's like a pot that cannot hold a cover

Because there is a thirst that is in you
That can never ever be quenched
A greed for everything in sight
Like a lust that can't be benched

See even if you had everything
You still would be searching for more
From every boundaries of the world
From the sea to shining shore

See sometimes you may sit and think
That the life you live is not fair
But there is one thing you must believe
That there's a love that really does care

He doesn't care about what you got
He doesn't care what you could win
The only thing He wants from you
Is a Christian life without sin

See each second that you live your life
And each moment you should pray
Every gift that I give to you
You will be blessed by giving it away

As you are welcomed to My kingdom
And you hear my angel's sweet melody
There is nothing here but true love
And there is no room for Jealousy

Terry Daniels

Love At First Sight

Love at first sight
How could this be?
I look at you
And you look at me

Is this by fate?
Or is this an illusion?
I know what I saw
And that is my conclusion

For me to have felt
That I had seen you before
A mystery in my future
That I must definitely explore

Because when things happen like this
There must be an explanation
We knew how we felt
Without any conversation

I can see me holding you
With a very gentle touch
A desire and a wonder
That I have longed for so much

With each second that I imagined
I must know even more
To penetrate into your life
And open up that closed door

You see I want to know
Everything that I can
To give you a world
And the heart of this man

You see with each time that I think of you
Rather it be day or night
To show you what real happiness is
Because it was truly Love at First Sight

Chanell

Chanell is a lady
How can I describe
Each second I am with her
I am so glad I am alive

As I look at her gorgeous face
There is nothing on Earth to compare
For the first time in my life
I found a true love for me to share

When I wake up each morning
And it will continue through the day
My thoughts and my heart is with her
Forever and always

You see because I cannot believe
That these butterflies are so real
This eternal love I have for her
All through my heart I can feel

You see this is so true
And I do know why
The only thing that I can think of
Is that beautiful blue sky

Because angels are around
And angels do exist
But for her to be in my life
There could be no greater gift

Because she is no fantasy
She is the beginning of all my dreams
For me to love her forever
There is no measure, there is no extreme

As I think of a true happiness
Only with her I can tell
There is no way that I could have imagine
My real love forever her name is Chanell

Shayna

Shayna, what is it about you
That I like so much?
Is it your smile, your walk?
Or just hoping for your touch?

You see lady when I first saw you
There was a twinkle in your eyes
You are a true blessing from the heavens
Only our father knows why

Someone like you
Every man should meet
You are a princess on this Earth
And I would gladly bow at your feet

As I wonder to myself
Where have you been so long?
Every man's real fantasy
They would gladly take you home

To keep you safe and warm
From any kind of situation
A life to share only with you
An eternal relation

You see dreams are only dreams
And some dreams do come true
But my happiness in my life
Must be shared with only you

To be there for you
Through all thick and thin
To show you a forever love
That has no end

For all of my life
I prayed for my soul mate to forever love
Then I finally met Ms. Perfect
Her name, Shayna

Chara

Chara what is it about you
That I notice you from a far?
More beautiful than any princess
And much brighter than any star

A lady that I see
A true angel that's within
A desire of every man
A true love that I must win

The things I notice about her
I must see each and every day
My happiness to share with her
Each second I do pray

This life that we will live
From one season to the next
A love from the heavens
Only our God could have blessed

The thoughts of her not with me
My heart does skip a beat
The best thing in my life
With you I am complete

Each adventure that I search
Each dream that I pursue
Each moment of my life
Must be spent only with you

Anything that I need
Any happiness I will have
Any time I feel down
Only you can make me laugh

As I look at my life with her
I will give her no sorrow
All the love in my heart
Will be shared only with Chara

Terry Daniels

Drop Dead Gorgeous

Drop dead gorgeous
How can this truly be?
To look at this beautiful lady
Then to look at me

So how can I be the luckiest
Man in this whole wide world
To even get to stand by you
Such a lovely girl

Is this for real?
Or is it my imagination
To even have a foolish thought
Of any kind of a relation

You see a fantasy is only a fantasy
And some of them do come true
But this eighth wonder of the world
In my heart I know that it is you

You see now I do understand
Where my future will begin
I will love her forever more
Only her heart that I must win

Because I would not comfort you
Unless I bring my best
Thousand percent of it all
Not one percent less

Because a lady like you
Comes only once in a million years
The thought of you even talking to me
My eyes could not hide the tears

As I have given my all to you
My love has grown enormous
For me to wake up every morning
To my woman who is Drop Dead Gorgeous

So Many Things

So many things
That I see in you
Like something so unreal
But something oh so true

It is like living in a dream
That you do not ever want to wake up from
Even though it is a fantasy
I can still feel your touch

Something so soft and sweet
That I have never felt before
A feeling all in me
That brings me so much joy

To caress only you
Over and over again
A lust that I must have
A love that I must win

Because I would know myself
That this will only happen one time
After it is all done
You most definitely must become mine

So you must take this chance
As it is presented
Because everybody gets only one
And that is the limit

Because this is the definition
Of what a true love really does
A part of you so precious and dear
She's your princess from above

As I love everything about you
To only you I gave this ring
That is just the start
Because there are So Many Things

Terry Daniels

Redemption

Redemption is something
That means payback for me
To get my revenge
So that I can be free

Free from that thing
That came into my life
Free from this pain
That I will make right

But now for me to feel
That you have stabbed me in the back
Now it is my turn
To return this attack

But this is a fight
That I won't fight alone
It is time to regroup
It is time to call home

To the place where the champ lives
He has all wins and not one loss
This prize fighter I speak of
He is the boss

He will pick you up always
Whenever you are down
He will fight all of your battles
Each one round by round

He will take that hate from you
And He will turn it in to love
He will protect all of you
Inside of his loving glove

No matter who tries to hurt you
There will never be any exemptions
Because you are My precious child
I will take care of all of your Redemption

Off the Chain

Off the chain is a phrase
To me it means out of control
No one you will listen to
No one to tell you your role

You see you think this is your world
And there is no one here but you
Anything that you want or say
It will always have to be true

You see as you wake up each morning
And it will continue throughout the day
This is exactly what will happen
And it will be only your way

You have feelings for not one thing
Not any respect for no one
This is what I say is right
This is what will be done

Now feel what I say is true
Because I don't understand
This world is not about you
And you are not God's plan

Who do you think you are?
What world are you from?
There is only one king
And that is the Father's Son

Because He died for everyone
So that we all could live
He did it for this whole wide world
For you eternal life He gives

Now as long as you live your life like that
One day there will be pain
Just call upon our Lord Jesus Christ
He will put you back On The Chain

Terry Daniels

Let's Go Fishing

Let's go fishing
To see what we can catch
No matter if it is only one
But I prefer it be a batch

See the place that we will go
The weather is just great
The sun will be shining bright
The time is not too late

You see this is what I enjoy
Because it is so real
Every time I pull one in
You can't imagine how I feel

To get one on your line
Is something that I can't describe
A rush that runs all through you
An emotion that you cannot hide

But this is something much more
Than just a simple event
This will last forever
That's why our Jesus was sent

To pull us in one by one
This thing it must be done
To understand how important this is
The Father sent His Son

See now is the time to get serious
And please use the right bait
Because if you miss just one cast
You might be just too late

See now it's time that the joking stops
And your soul must begin to listen
See this is the time the Father will appear
So Let Us All Go Fishing

This is For Me

This is for me
No matter whatever I choose
This choice is in my face
Either to win or to lose

Because this is my life
And I am alone to do as I please
I can take things seriously
Or I can just tease

You see this is the first time
That I can think only for me
Because I have no burdens
I am just free

As I wake up each morning
My day has no plans
Anything I want to do
It will not be in demand

Because I don't have no time
Or clock to live by
I can do as I want
And do not have to answer why

Now what kind of person
That would think that is true
Anybody that thinks like that
They really are a fool

Because this is a world
That has changed all directions
It needs a relationship
With true love and affections

So with my life, my body, and soul
I give it all to Thee
To live in my Father's Kingdom forever
Now This is For Me

Terry Daniels

Anything Can Happen Will Happen

Anything can happen and will happen
This is so very true
Some things that is very strange to others
It can become strange to you

But this is a world
That has its both ups and downs
One second you are happy as a lark
The next one you look like a clown

So understand this one thought
Your life will go through changes
So with that thought on your mind
It will be subject to certain arranges

So the only thing that you can do
Is to take each step in stride
Now please remember this simple thought
You can run but you can't hide

Because whatever does happen
It does it for a purpose
But you must also remember
If you go to the bottom you will surface

Because there is a hand that will grab you
Through all of your disappointment and problems
The answer to all of your solutions
Just call His name and He will be able to solve them

Because you are the reason
That He came to this Earth
To return to you your legacy
That was given to you before birth

You see whenever you get upset
And your mouth starts snapping
Just turn it all over to God
He can stop Anything That Can and Will Happen

Fake

Fake to me means
No good all wrong
It has no purpose here
It does not belong

Now why would you want something?
In your life that's not true?
If it is not authentic
Then what good is it to you?

But there is a thing
That is real as your life
Something that will take care of
All of your troubles and strifes

Because when you come to this world
You were not alone
There was a presence that's with you
That will never steer you wrong

Just ask and believe
It will come in instant
No matter the location
No matter the distant

So open up your heart
Because your life is right here
There are angels all around you
So you should have no fear

Please remember one thing
Your purpose here is real
A true love all around you
A Father that you can feel

There's a serenity of love about you
Just ask the Lord your soul to take
If there was ever a reality
Well then know our Father is No Fake

Terry Daniels

Rumor

Rumor is something
That will come from behind
Something that you don't know of
But this rumor will shine

As I sit here and I think
Of what is really clear
This rumor I speak of
Could show love and also fear

Fear in a way
That you cannot trust no one
But there is a love in my life
The love of my Father's son

You see He is always there
No matter what you would expect
A love He has given you
A true love with no regret

To know of this love
That I know that is within
A love with all powers
A love with no sins

A love so mystic
That I cannot describe
A love that smiles at you
A love that doesn't hide

It is there each morning
And it continues through the night
With each breath that you take
It is right there insight

As I think of what comes out of man's mouth
There can be so much humor
But out Lord Jesus Christ
Is No Rumor

Eternity

Eternity is a life
That is forever and a day
A life that only our Lord
Can show you the way

A way that They had planned
From the beginning of time
To show us their love
Their true love so divine

To love something so much
That only they could understand
This vision that they had
So they created a man

As I think and I wonder
And this I have no doubt
Their love so glorious and so wonderful
That only they could share out

I am writing this poem
For my grandmother
A lady so special
That I would choose no other

The love that she gave me
I won't even try to describe
Every day and every night
I wish that she was alive

But the Father gave her something
Much stronger than my love
He gave her happiness
Something much greater above

But this is a life
That we will understand free
So thank you my Father
For this Eternity

Terry Daniels

Material

Material is things
That is man made
But as we all do know
These things will eventually fade

See you can buy it one day
Then the next day exchange it
Now this one that you purchased
You grow to like it bit by bit

This tool that you bought
Was it worth what you paid?
There was a refund
A receipt that you should have saved

Because without that paper
It cannot be returned
The money that you spent
The money that you earned

Because when they said forever
They did mean forever
The stamp placed on it
Was through any and all weather

Now please listen very carefully
There is something that will never expire
This thing last for eternity
Forever free never a buyer

You see it cannot be sold
And it comes from above
Paid for in full
By the Lord Jesus' blood

So for all the rich and well off
That thinks their life is inferial
My Father's house has no room
For none of your Materials

To Forgive and to Forget

To forgive and to forget
Can this be true?
Only this question can be answered
And it's only by you

Because if anyone hurts you
How would you feel?
Was it an accident?
Or was it for real?

Because this did hurt
And it caused so much pain
That day the sun was shining bright
The next second it was falling rain

You see things can happen unexpected
There was no reason for it to be
But now it's real and it won't go away
Now I must face it so I can be free

But this is a life that
Everything you ask isn't always done
Because one little victory in battle
Doesn't mean that the war is won

Now just think back when Jesus came
How did He really feel?
To come here for you and me
To sign this everlasting deal

Because without Jesus
Our lives would have an end
But with the Son of God
He delivered us from all sins

For our Lord Jesus Christ to come to this world
To pay for our eternal debt
For Him to hang from the cross
Please follow His lead to Forgive and to Forget

Well Represented

Well represented
Everybody would like to hear
To do what you are suppose to
And to not have no fear

To take what you are asked
And to do it with no problem
Even if it's not right
You will find a way to solve them

You see this is a position
That not everyone can hold
Something that calls for authority
This means a leading role

To take on a position
To tell others what to do
A job not for everyone
Only just a few

Now trust me and believe this
What I am about to say
There is only one real leader
And He is with you every day

No matter what can develop
Anything seen and unseen
There is a love all around you
That is real and is no dream

As I think of our Father
All of the promises you thought were hinted
Now just look at His resume
I would say He was Well Represented

Grey

Grey is a word
That is between time and space
You must understand
Now look at these times, then except what you face

Because if you choose black
Then to not know of white
There could be something better
That you didn't know was insight

To judge one thing
Then not see the other
There could be something wrong
So you must look even further

See as I sit here
I can think of only one place
The home that I have lived for
That started all human races

To look in to your heart
And not to know of a true life
There is someone that knows
Of all your troubles and strife

As He gave life to both Adam
Then to Eve
He knew in His heart
There would be troubles to receive

But being an image of Him
He did understand
Not to know wrong from right
It would be amongst all man

Now to get to the point
He will show you the right way
Just trust and believe in Him
And there will be no Grey

Terry Daniels

What a Joyous Day

What a joyous day
For me to get to see
A place of tranquility
A place that I feel free

Free from things
That I have left behind
To search for a better place
A new peace of mind

My worries are not here
And my troubles are gone
A foundation that I feel
A place to call home

You see this world was designed
To share happiness and love
With anything you don't know
All your answers will come from above

You see the Father does know
Of all of the things that you go through
With each step that you take
You are always in his view

Because this path that you take
You will always have a guide
There will be a presence of love
That will never try to hide

It will be with you each morning
And it will show you the way
A voice that will be with you
All you have to do s just pray

As I sit here and I think
There are no words that I can say
As I gave it all to my Father
Man what a Joyous Day

What Would Make Me Happy

What would make me happy?
And this is what I feel
I am opening up my heart
So then you know that I am real

Because there are other people
That I love more than myself
Just having them in my life
That is my true wealth

You see what I feel for them
There are no words to describe
By me being their Father
I am so glad to be alive

You see they are a part of me
That only our Father's goodness could do
To show me and this world
That His love is very true

You see this thing inside of me
There are so many emotions to explore
This feeling I have for my family
Each day I love them even more

Because they are my reason
That I push myself to the extreme
With this goal in my heart
That I Will Follow My Dream

With the help from my sons
And the Lady I made My Wife
This vision that I am seeing
Is becoming as realistic as life

You see once upon a time
I was cruel, mean, and very snappy
Then once I gave it all to the Father
Now I understand what Would Make Me Happy

Terry Daniels

Everybody Wants Power

Everybody wants power
And why is that so
So they can veto
That small word called no

For it to have two little letters
It carries a lot of weight
Because anytime you want something done
It's best not to be late

See you can think you are in control
Of all situations
No matter if they are enemies
Or very close relations

You see this would be the thing
That you would have programmed in your mind
Because you will know the out come
Because you set the time

Because if they don't do it right
Then what good are they to you
You see if these people are not like me
They most definitely will not see my view

Now see if this was the reason
Why this world was created
It never would have been done
Not even illustrated

You see the Father who made this
Made everyone equal
Because with His food for thought
There would never be a sequel

As I look around at this world
I see the birds, grass, and the flowers
To make all of these things alive
Only our God controls All Power

Patience

Patience is a virtue
As everybody says
To understand this though
It will come in different ways

It may come when you want it
Or it may not come at all
It could come in the spring
Or may be in the fall

But no matter when it comes
You still must wait
It could be around the corner
Or it could be very late

To have this thing on your mind
You can't be happy until it's done
A matter that's out of your control
The sitting is no fun

Now please listen to me
And I hope you do understand
There's a clock that times all of your prayers
And it's a part of the master plan

You see there may be times
When it seems nothing will go your way
And there's no one who really cares
Just think back when you were a child and just start to pray

Because when all doors seem closed
And there's no light to come in
Remember a love on Calvary
Who died for all of our sins

Now just imagine something smooth and desirable
That brings you such a warm sensation
Just give your life to our Father
Because He has been very Patient

Terry Daniels

God is Good

God is good
That is oh so true
He loves this whole world
And not just a few

When He first thought
Of all off the darkness around Him
He put together a plan
That was not a whim

Something that He had thought about
For a very long time
So He put it all together
Slowly in His mind

Then He decided the dark
It had to go
So He brought in the sun
To brighten up the show

Then the birds and the bees
The flowers and the grass
Everything that He gave life
His vision that will last

But one day He decided
To go even further
To bring forth human life
Like no one other

But then as time went by
His beautiful creation had changed
All His love that He had put here
It all turned to pain

As He looked all around for something true
And there was nothing that He could find
So His Son gave His life for our sins
God is Good All the Time

Please Do It For Me

Please do it for me I am so upset
And very scared
A friend of mine is sick
But she won't say a word

The things that she has done
Not even a good friend would have tried
But everything I would ask her
Not once would she try to hide

I would put her in situations
That I did not see a way out
But she would do it completely
And there would be no doubt

Because she is so much
A very big part of my life
She was the only person that believed
Who helped put my vision to sight

Every time I see her
There is always a smile on her face
With that thought planted in my mind
It will never ever be erased

Her family that she supports
I know that she gives her all
Because she is the kind of lady
There is nothing too short or tall

Because she is the kind of person
That she will always give her best
A true angel of yours my Father
I know she is heavenly blessed

So Father as I ask you sincerely
Please set all her troubles free
A princess that I care for dearly
Please Do It For Me

Feed Me

Feed me
The things that is good for me
Feed me the things
That will make me see

To see where the darkness
Can turn to light
To know of a new beginning
That will come insight

To understand this world
Why does it exist?
To think of a creation
That has a list

Now Father as I sit here
My curiosity must know
I know that you are a friend
And not a foe

Because you are the answer
To any question that will arrive
Like why am I here
Why am I alive

Because there is nothing before you
So you have no past
Now I understand my present
And a new life that will last

So Father I pray
For everything that I receive
To love you forever
Please my Lord Feed Me

What Is This?

What is this my Lord?
This thing that I feel
Why is it my Lord
For this thing to be real

Because what I see
Are not the things I was told
The things that I thought of
Those things of pure gold

Father I ask you
Where did I go wrong?
This emptiness in my heart
Makes me feel so all alone

Father what is the problem?
Please make me understand
I know this was not your dream
I know this was not Your plan

Now as you speak to Me my child
I do know what to say
You must trust and believe in Me
Most definitely you must pray

No matter what you may think
This is for only a short time
You must keep your faith in Me
And my king Dome you will find

See when this world was created
I loved you oh so much
The journey that was in front of you
I knew it would be rough

See when this nightmare is over
And then will get your wish
And you finally see all the miracles of My heaven
Now you can say What Is This

Terry Daniels

Player

Player is a word
That only they understand
This word to them
Not only a woman also a man

To know of this word
You must know you
To know in your mind
That this feeling is true

As you look at one thing
You also see another
But to love one person
You are also looking further

But to look and know
That this is all about me
And for them to understand
I will always be free

For them to understand
That I will never commit
For them to realize
That this is all they will get

But for me to feel
I feel no pain
But for me as a player
I must have this fame

But as I think of this world
I can feel so much
To have this special person
That only I want to touch

As I kiss you and love you
I taste this special flavor
And to know that I love you
I can no longer be a Player

More Than Enough

More than enough
Is all that I need
That part is done
Now I must believe

Now just sit back and imagine
Everything that you want is in one place
Your happiness and desires
All in one space

To look at a woman
That is more beautiful than any picture
A verse in my heart
An everlasting scripture

You see everything that I would hope for
Out of my wildest dreams
You are my total package of love
My star light and my queen

You have opened up my heart
To things I've never known
You have presented me with a passion
That has never been shown

Each time that I think of you
My hear does skip a beat
Such an enormous high
That no one else could compete

A life that I must share
Only with you
I will give you all of me
Baby my love forever true

Because with you my princess
Only you will I lust
But you know and I know
That you are More Than Enough

My World is Complete

My world is complete
Now that I found you
No more wandering where
No one else to pursue

Because everything I desire
Is all in one form
My soul mate from heaven
Even before I was born

My life that was planned
With only your true love to give
Happiness on this Earth
For the two of us to live

Because with you by my side
There are no stars we can't reach
Not a challenge in front of us
Only our happiness to seek

A life to live together
Each day one at a time
As I hold you ever so gently
And to know that you are mine

To caress your soft body
To feel your special touch
To know in my heart
That I love you so much

You see there are words inside of me
That I cannot get out
But my feelings for you forever
Will never change; no doubt

So whatever else could I ask for?
All my standards you meet
My life is not perfect
My World is Complete

Till Death Do Us Part

Till death do us part
This is what I know
My lonely days are over
I have found my rainbow

This has been rough and hard
And a very lonely time
For me to truly believe
A real lady is finally mine

Yes, you are here
And you are here to stay
A lady for only me to love
Forever and a day

Because all of my waiting
Is finally all gone
My relentless hunt is over
You are right where you belong

To be with me today
And I promise tomorrow
To love you unconditionally
And to never bring you no sorrow

Before you there was no one
That even had a clue
That I was such a lonely man
And waiting only for you

You see when I found you
My whole life was fulfilled
A love to live together
Only happiness for us to live

So baby I love you so much
To only you I give my heart
I will be there with you
Till Death Do Us Part

Terry Daniels

I Want You Back

I want you back
This I do not believe
I thought I had another happy
But I was truly deceived

How can you improve on perfection?
Anything else is no equal
But with me and my dumb mentality
I thought I could find a sequel

So what can I do now?
I do not have an answer
A poison that is eating up my heart
Like an incurable cancer

I know that I cannot
Turn back the hands of time
Even if I could do so
You, I would not find

You see a good lady comes very seldom
And you were that one
For me to have one more chance
There is no way under this sun

You see my turn for happiness came
For the first time in my life
A lady that stood by my side
And understood the word sacrifice

Whenever I would feel down and out
She would gently hold my hand
To show me and this whole world
That I will always be her man

And now this day has come
And I was praying for it to be an act
But as she slowly walked away
Baby please, I Want You Back

I Really Miss You

I really miss you
So very much
The smile on your pretty face
The softness of your loving touch

Because never did think
That I could hurt so bad
When I asked you to Marry me
I thought it would last

Because each morning that I get up
I feel so all alone
The house is oh so empty
This is not a loving home

I am feeling so depressed
I don't know where to turn
I never thought this would happen
Now without you I must learn

Because this was not to happen
It never was part of my plan
Now without you Ms. Lady
Alone I must stand

So what can I do?
To get over this hurt
The tears keep falling from my eyes
And that don't seem to work

I am trying so hard to get over you
And it's hurting me so much to lose
With all the ladies in the world
You are the only one I did choose

As I walk around in my lonely world
And baby I know this is true
Without the only real love that was in my life
Darling I Really Miss You

Terry Daniels

It's All For You

It's all for you
All of my dreams and desires
With you on my mind
I am always reaching higher

Because there is no way
That I can feel I gave my all
No matter how big it is
Or no matter how small

You see there are no limitations
On the things I would like to see you with
See the world would be your playground
All the knowledge would be you gift

But this is what life is for
There are things you need to know about
This world is not all cut and dry
There forever will be doubts

Just look even further my friend
And please try to understand
There's a love that is needed in our lives
And it is in great demand

To protect and stay by your side
No matter from what or who
It's only purpose in life
Is to take good care of you

See if you have problems
And you don't know where to turn
There is something that will show you hope
And a deep wondering of concern

No matter what this world may say
My love forever will be true
With any accomplishment that I achieve
In my life It's All For You

Favor to Me

Favor to me
What does it mean?
Something that shows respect
Something that's not green

You see there are things in life
That you cannot always buy
Money is not always the answer
Money can be denied

To be honest and trustworthy
Because His word does stand
It's something that wasn't given to Him
It is something that He had planned

Because this is your life
It should be simple and smooth
With one wrong step
Everything that you had you could loose

See you must be careful
On the things that you decide
There could be a price with it
A secret you can't hide

You see there is something in your life
That what you see is what you get
It will always give you more
And it will never give you less

Now understand what I am saying
And believe me this is true
There is a passion and a desire
That wants to be only with you

You see there is a delight on your menu
That once you taste it you must savor
A love that will give you unconditional
Everlasting Favor

Terry Daniels

About Face

About face
What does that mean?
Something that you must do
To fulfill this dream

Because it started where
I thought that I should go
As I continued to walk
The walk became very slow

But then I decided
That this did not look right
The path that I was walking
Became the darkness of night

So then I stopped
And I knew this was the wrong way
So I turned to my Father
And I started to pray

Father I am lost
So please help me out
With all of my faith
And I still have no doubt

That You are the only one
Who knows how I feel
Please show me Your light
So I know this is real

For me to know and understand
That only Your love is true
For you to believe me, Father
That I trust and love only You

Because You are my Savior
Who created this whole race
As I give my soul to you my Lord
Now I will About Face

For Real, For Real

For real, for real
Is this the truth?
You should have learned this
Since you were a youth

A growing process
That should stay with you for life
It should always be with you
Every day and every night

To know the difference
Between right and wrong
To know the place
Where each one belongs

Because this is your life
And you will be liable for your actions
The results that you should get
They should be to your satisfaction

Because everything you do
Other people will see
The things that you put out there
Are what others will believe

Because if you are a fake
The real you will show
And everyone that you are around
Eventually they will know

So if you lose the trust
Of anyone you are around
A dishonest reputation
Will be what you would have found

Now please understand this thought
Because this is not let's make a deal
We really need our Father
And this is For Real, For Real

Terry Daniels

Spare the Rod and Spoil the Child

Spare the road and spoil the child
What does that really mean?
A problem in your life
That's what t would seem

Because to discipline anyone
There must be a problem
A solution that should be around
A remedy to solve them

You see things are not always
What they should be
Because sometimes you must look closer
And then you can see

As I think to myself
That two wrongs don't make a right
Because whatever it is
There is someone who will fight

For your salvation of love
That you must truly learn
A respect for your life
That you must truly earn

But this is your life
And how so soon we forget
A love that loves you
That paid all of your debts

Where all burdens are none
And all troubles don't exist
A world that has everything
There is no reason for you to wish

As I look at this world
Can't you see the last mile?
Now it's the time for everyone to wake up
And not Spare the Rod and to Spank the Child

Now is The Time

Now is the time
For this real dream to come true
This thing that was started
This vision was for only you

For you to take your blessing
That only the Father could give
To follow the path He laid out
For you and your family to live

Because everyone was born
With one particular thing to do in life
It might be to run the world
Or maybe just take a wife

You see all decisions that you make
Is your choice to chose
Because the one that you pick
Could be the main one that you loose

No matter what you decide to do
Make sure it is what you want
You see this should be your life's dream
So don't be afraid to hunt

You see this is your future
And you should live it day by day
To get your promotion jump started
You must remember to always pray

Because all the things that you desire in life
There is only one place you can get it done
The big blue sky on top of the world
The home of the Father and Son

Now as I started my journey
With all the reputations and research I had to find
As I look at the start of my rainbow
Now is the Time

Terry Daniels

If Only You Knew

If only you knew
What's on my mind
Something so different and unusual
That I truly must find

It's there inside of me
Always 24-7
My only relief is
That I must find heaven

Because that is the place
Where all problems are solved
There is nothing on Earth
That can't be resolved

When things come into your life
And you don't know where to turn
There's a love all around you
That has a great amount of concern

You see no matter what burdens
That you will endure
There is an angel always with you
And that you can get rest assure

To protect and guide you
And show you the right way
An answer so easy
All you must do is just pray

He will keep His word
Because His word is true
Like I've said so many times
His true love is you

For all of these doubters
That doesn't have a clue
There's a life that you can have forever
If Only You Knew

Genuine

Genuine is something
That's for real and for sure
A thing that is authentic
This thing is so pure

You will know that it's different
Because it will be like no other
Once it is destroyed
It can never be recovered

Sometimes you may get lucky
And find something so close
It's like touching a vision
And holding on to a ghost

It's like living a dream
That stays constantly on your mind
Or wishing on a star
For something that you won't find

You see these things that you think
They are already in your face
Everything that you desire
All in one place

This place that I speak of
Can grant any dreams you could imagine
A paradise so close
That's right over the horizon

You can live there forever
And everything is free
The home of Jesus Christ
And His Father that we call Thee

So if you want something so unique
And priceless that you can find
Just turn to our God
He is most definitely Genuine

Terry Daniels

What's Next?

What's next for me?
I really don't know
The only thing that I will do
Is to stay on this straight road

So what is my purpose?
Please make me understand
What are your reasons?
What are your plans?

Please listen very carefully
There are only simple things you must d
To know and to believe that
All my love is for you

You see before you were ever born
I knew what you would be
The world did not know
And you did not see

This journey that you are traveling
May seem long and very hard
Now understand that's what faith is
You must trust your God

Because I am there with you
Even when you are a sleep
There is not a burden to big
Or a well to deep

There is nothing in your life
That I cannot change
You see I created the sunshine
And only I can make it rain

So My child accept
And know you have been blessed
Because only I, your Father, knows
For sure What's Next

OTHER TITLES BY MR DANIELS

LET'S HAVE FUN   **2008**

About the Author

Mr. Daniels is a nationally recognize poet, after his highly acclaimed freshman release "Just Have Fun". He currently resides in Statesville, NC.

Made in the USA
Lexington, KY
04 March 2013